As the trees have grown

As the trees have grown

Stephanie de Montalk

TE HERENGA WAKA
UNIVERSITY PRESS

Te Herenga Waka University Press
Victoria University of Wellington
PO Box 600 Wellington
teherengawakapress.co.nz

ISBN 978-1-77692-077-8

A catalogue record is available from the National Library
of New Zealand

Printed by Ligare, Auckland

For John, my jo, John

Contents

Can any vital process take place
without something being changed?

Marcus Aurelius, *Meditations*

1

Heartfelt

The rolling slopes and groves
of my lissom, evergreen heart,

struck by the dysfunction of left
ventricular damage—etymology

uncertain but doubtless virally
loaded—were at imminent risk

of fatal erosion. The physician
disengaged her stethoscope and

polished its chest piece, checked
her profile in a reflective button

and suggested transfer to critical
care in the city at four the next

morning on a small propeller-
powered plane. She confirmed

admission to a unit illuminated
by the echoes and reverberations

of cardiac musculature in motion,
flexed her fingers, flicked a switch

and murmured, 'But first a little
music, and scrutiny of the beat

and rhythmic integrity of your
waltzing and fox-trotting heart?'

Simple physics

Seeking
a source,

a cause,
a cure,

I encountered the restorations
of memory

and replacements
of imagination:

relief as vivid
and varied

as random dice
tiered

in pairs;
spinning coins

spaced
with momentum

and gravity;
flat stones

flicked over
taut water—

otiose,
lightly poised

at the edge
of oncoming rain

waiting to quiver
and drop softly.

Fixed wing

The early morning
medevac plane

shuddered
during lift-off,

stalled on the parapet
of a cloud castle

and crabbed through
crosswinds

commandeering
the graphs

mapping passengers'
heart rates,

body heat,
oxygen saturations

and—in the glare
of touchdown lights

from the runway—
the insistent

lilac shading
of fingertips

and lips denoting
the mottled loss

of peripheral
circulation.

Orientation

I entered the ward
cautiously, as nurses

levered the struggling
strands of what

appeared to be
weeds from tilted

beds of staked peas
and runner beans

with small sharp
hoes, and hid

the limp remnants
in the lees

of large, late
flowering globe

artichokes—
notwithstanding

the camouflage
cache's tendency

to suffocation by
soil saturation

and compaction in
an absence of life-saving

grit and sand,
should spring rains
           fail to drain.

Distraction

Curtain swish.
Pen click.

Wrist grip.
Murmurs.

*

Mules, tormented
by horseflies,

ruminated
exhausted

on the Rock of Gibraltar—
too weak

to flick their tails,
twist their necks,

swing their heads
and stand motionless—

until the mud
I had smeared

on their legs caked,
and the bundles

of straw I had warmed
and pressed

against the bellies
of the patient,

obedient beasts
gave relief.

*

'Ticking?'
'Like clockwork.'

ASA 400

That week, seasonally
inspired birds

were zooming
and swooping

in platoons more
than four stories tall.

A red-headed parakeet
was ablaze

in the eucalyptus tree.
Wrens inspected

the visibility
and strategic importance

of roosts
in the ngaio.

The neighbour's sulphur-
crested, lock-picking

cockatoo bloomed
beyond the laddered

reach of the oak's
stately crown.

And a kea deserted
its worm-rich patch

of organic soil to ride light
waves across the lawn's

peaty surface
to the glabrous shade

of the laurel bay,
where a camera—

single lens reflex
with shutter speed

priority—filmed
day for night,

and night for day,
hidden in a scratchy nest

of dry moss
and kindling.

*

Also noted,
a miscalculated

ketamine infusion
leading to an encounter

with the shadowy
form of a kākā

staring defiantly,
side-eyed, as it

pecked at the insect-
proof mesh and bullet-

resistant render
of the intensive care

unit door, awaiting
arrival of an olive

brown, air-thudding,
master-key-carrying

army of compatriots—
large twilight moths

with harsh scarlet
underwings,

ready to empty
the contents

of the Dangerous Drugs
cabinet into carrier bags,

and tear through the air,
like explosions.

All night

Nymph skins clung
to ponga trunks,

and clumps of yellow
and black spraxia

denounced the creek's
dwindling tide mark

as if through trumpets.
Knee-deep in summer

heat and cicada rasps
of survival, I positioned

pots of common lavender
and false heather

around the daylit
perimeter.

2

Allurement

Last weekend the wind
brought cobalt skies,

bright hills and cicadas
louder than you're likely

to remember them.
The cats slept in fresh grass,

leaves swirled
on the lower lawn,

and all day there was
a deep, white light

and everything
with an edge to it.

Papaver somniferum

for Brittany Peck

I searched for Aunti Emma
in the treescapes of Asia,

carrying neither firearm
nor blade of purple-tipped

elephant grass for protection:
only a steely expression,

confirming an intention
to follow the coordinates

fixed by my guide
to the wind-shaped

trunks of the forests'
bristlecone pines with

the nails of fate
secreted in the linings

and poacher's pockets
of her tunic and hacking jacket.

*

I clambered in pursuit
of promising leads

across surface roots
and wet rocks,

dodging rainbow showers
of lepidopterans unsettled

by the guide's pounding
installations and throaty

instructions. If there were
freshwater springs to be found,

I swam in the midday heat,
and bathed in the cool

of evening before
revoking the lamp's guttering

haze and sharing a dose
of the day's medicinal

purchase—smoked, nibbled
raw, or mixed with rum

and sipped as the harvest
of excitement and danger,

and pleasure and remorse
upon which the tincture's

rhythm revealing the continuum
of smoke and mirrors depends.

You will touch down

in spring
to feverish winds

and sheet-white light
from Antarctica,

and find that as
the trees have grown

so, too, the boxy
twin-engine congregations

of kererū—air ferries
of the species—

and the delicate nests
of tītipounamu

wherein each tiny rifleman
claims less than one gram—

the looped space and weight
of a paperclip.

Yes, spring—

typically
persistent,

whether troubling
the dip and swell

of the Great Southern Ocean,
or buffeting

the purplish-black
berry-fruit

of the *Fuchsia
excorticata*—

not yet in season
although delicious

mixed with jam
and eaten raw.

*

Tūī with white
tufted throats—

necks craned,
beaks agape,

brushy-tipped tongues
lapping

and extracting
nectar—

will swing
from blossom

to blossom,
accosting their

turbulent settings
and thickening

their familiar
momentums

with staccato trilling
and clicking.

Amor fati

Such a long haul
for a brown trout:
travel by steam train

in the tender behind
the engine, sightless
in the water tank

evading the pipe
to the boiler,
iron flakes gripping

your gills, and irritations
of steel and steam
interrupting your lateral

lines and muddling
the clarity of your
acoustic scene,

*

when you might
have coasted between
the banks of sand

and white, daisy-
rich kaolin clay,
strumming the upswing

of a tidal wash,
before your transfer—
nose to tail

like an eel
into a fire bucket's
galvanised clank,

and pressed against
the rhythm of the driver's
testy stride from

busy platform
to noisy street,
to monotonous,

thinly carpeted
overnight room
where, in the embrace

of Epictetus, Seneca
and Marcus Aurelius,
you will round out

Stoic acceptance
of full life experience
from this day's unadorned

pre-dawn start
in the north
to this evening's

sprinkle-fed meal
and equally rough
and tumble affairs,

as determined by
the weight and nature
of fate in the south.

Events

Mindful of atmospheric rivers of rain
and other phenomenal events in the sky—

white peacocks, for instance, neither
here nor there in the mist, lamenting

their loss of identity and facility
for fanning spectacular eye-laden tails,

or giraffes confessing to cardiac stress
caused by pumping their small,

super-charged hearts at industrial
heights during installations of scaffolding

and signage, and verifications of the
matchstick vulnerabilities of softwoods.

What to do but bake bread and brew tea
before the occurrences peak and the house

is without power, and contain the cat,
likely to be panicked by changes

in barometric pressure or by the risk
of finding itself locked

in a box labelled QUANTUM MECHANICS,
updating Schrödinger on the blurring of

scientific theory—specifically, the feasibility
of declaring a cat, or peacock or giraffe, sealed

from view, alive and dead at the same time—
who may by now be irretrievable behind the

polyester cotton of the Daily Wash in the front
loading machine. More convenient, surely, to

secure shutters, air-lock storm doors, gaffer-
tape window panes in matte black and, sedated

by a glass of pomegranate juice (pip-free),
and the instantly realised verbal imagery

and craftsmanship of *The Poems of Nizami*
(hardback edition in salmon-pink fabric),

take the by now hazy staircase to bed, cognisant
as you settle for the night that the flooding

and thrumming of wind-rippling river storms,
magnified by punctilious tearings of air, iron,

timber and tin, will be assuaged when,
having cleaned the spark plugs

and tweaked the starter motor
of its locked box, you picture the cat

(and, if appropriate, the pallid peacock and heart-
starved giraffe) heading at speed (alive or possibly

not) toward dawn, with the earth orbiting the sun
in the burnished benediction of a gold and orange horizon.

Trance

Polished panelling.
Lamp gleam.

Carrara marble
in shadow.

The jade elephant
from Hong Kong

on the bookcase,
its stained ear

out of sight,
its cracked trunk

in escape mode
facing the length

of traditionally designed
hand-printed cotton

stamped ESFAHAN,
importing

the immensity
of the late-afternoon

silence in Shah Square
as pale rays

of red sun
saturated

the hills,
subsuming,

with word-turning
purpose,

the sky's reflections.
We heard neither

gasps of admiration
nor ecstatic interpretations

of radiance that afternoon—
only the sighs

of wind-blown sand
awakening our

desert thirsts
to the marvellous.

3

From the Stoa

You switched off your motor,
clicked the car door,

crunched the gravel path
to the painted porch

and familiar crumble
of stucco

unencumbered
by colour,

before pausing
at the scorched

northern window
and the scent

of a twig
petrified forever

in a gap
between opening and closing.

Open terrain

Mid-morning blew
through the valley,

popping broom
in the grip of its heat.

Leggy gorse
scratched the hillside.

An agapanthus
in full bloom

berated and headed off
the letterbox,

and stalks of dry
fennel, the gate.

Decoction of Futurism

The day was a prototype
of its kind:

dandelions,
birds,

a buttery sun,
the absence

of snakes,
biting ants

and Futurist strips
of cirrus

wrestling themselves
into trousers—

as Vladimir Mayakovsky
may have encountered

the perfectly
pitched sky

and bespoke mode
of the clouds.

Outlier

Dominating the back lawn
and easing its wintry disposition,

the plain grace and promotional
intensity of the greywacke garden

path maintained the photogenic
appeal of the copper beech

(thin and pale in straitening age),
and enhanced the woody,

lichen-encrusted kōwhai (no longer
stunning in green and gold,

come spring and summer),
as resolutely as an ecstasy of tūī

releasing a gale-entrapped cone
from the crown of a junior spruce.

Imperium

We retrieved the house key
buried in oil cloth

from the waxy leaf drop
of the last wilding pine.

*

In daylight, the conifer
reached sylvan-high distance;

at night, its outline
whitened the moon;

and when turbulence
roared through its riggings

and ripped blue and green
through its crown,

and it pitched and rolled
like a stand-alone ship

on a perpendicular sea,
ejecting nests

and drawing needles
and seeds into the eye-

locking whirl, its habit
of dancing while rocking

itself into a dream
invited orchestration,

choreography,
an operatic score.

Keyboard or flute,
we wondered,

air conducting
the trunk's

unassailable rise
from the earth,

the branches'
unequivocal impressions

of movement and spread,
the pizzicato patter of dust

on the scene-setting
understories

of ferns and small shrubs.
Gregorian chant

or recitative?
Massed choir

or spot-lit
solo performance?

The grace of long
gliding strides

or a glissandi
of light, rapid steps?

In passing

With a key in the lock,
the house shimmied

and opened up to hand-
sanded floors teeming

with reindeer and floppy-
eared mountain hares

wrangling the stripes
of Siberian tigers.

*

In the kitchen: a round-
bodied brining barrel

awash with a mulberry
and date soup;

a pair of frugivorous bats
inclined to neurological

toxicity following excessive
consumption of cycad seeds;

a handful of cherries on
a fruit platter exciting

the dullard skin of a plum;
a jarred peach, glazed

with syrup,
masking a smashed avocado's

cruciferous tint; and, in
a reflection from the orchard

side of the window, a kererū—
hefty, red-eyed,

shuffling along a branch,
stretching its rainbow neck,

and beckoning from a corner
of the glass pane with its beak.

A very fine bird

During the long
weeks of sun

directly overhead,
torpor, hard-pressed

to our temples,
faced us down.

All the while,
the locally known

rock pigeon,
flaunting ownership

of the ridge
above our eaves,

strutted,
flicked his tail,

stirred his nondescript
plumage,

laid out sticks,
paid careless homage

to the recalibration
of twigs

and noisily positioned
his fittings:

plunking them down,
thumping,

nudging,
retrieving,

careening and cooing
to the beat

of his fervid
imagination.

After the rains broke

Flood tides arrived.
Rivers overflowed.

Creeks stalked the undergrowth.
Clay and shale separated.

*

Through the window,
the ghost gum was

entombed within
the cloaked stems

of the same neighbourly
vine choking the oak's

stolid branch-work,
and pitching handfuls

of hard fruit
into haversacks, at pace.

*

Campers stowed
biddable awnings

and multi-roomed tents.
Gardeners relinquished

the shoulder-tip shade
of triangular hats.

And farmers stirring
honey into hot milk

at midnight, held
their breaths

as they pored over
climate almanacs,

finessing the impact
of rain drops on erosion-

prone slopes, and spreading
sediment, silt and girting

rocks into certitudes
of slate-grey relief.

Cautious optimism

In thrall to the connections
of contact tracing,

whereby the relativity
of Einsteinian ideals

met the oblique flickers
of twilight on rust,

bidding opened online
featuring a succession

of vintage wrought-iron
pumps—freshly lacquered,

newly motorised,
flooded with the bodkin

and thread of recently acquired
scintillation and verve.

Photographed astride
water-logged lawns,

the dogged pumps
reached, then shirked,

their reserves in favour
of publication as

balancing and bonding
agents in centrespreads

relative to forthcoming
editions of *Entre Cour et Jardin*—

despite evidence,
sparingly shared,

of the pumps' less than
impressive ejection fractions.

Park life

for Belinda Ricketts

In summer
we see them

from the turret—
the British Blues—

lying in the grass
on the banks

of the Kumutoto Stream,
asleep in the secret

forest of rangiora,
rimu,

nikau
and makomako

above the motorway,
curled

like ponga
fronds,

long like
agapanthus petals.

*

Between times,
brushed by fragrant

viburnum
grandiflorum,

and in line
with the exactitude

of a single-stroke
Shrewsbury Clock,

they will settle indoors,
sharing an armchair

and the view
from the window

as the world's smallest airport
scrambles to produce

some semblance of a plot
involving the non–towered

tarmac, wind speed,
and permission to issue

muddy puddle advisories.
The Blues groom

themselves
and wave their tails,

paw pads cool
and clover damp,

cobby bodies
and amber eyes

dense with velvet
complacency.

4

The far north

Does the sea still sing in summer,
blue between the dusty hills

and northern sky, cloudless
and cicada strong on the gravel

road to Paihia? Does the sand
still skip along a line of surf,

and cartwheel over stones
and shells, and shine silver

cool and mirror-smooth on
beaches filled with children?

*

I dream of evenings soft and green,
of woollen sleeves and yellow lamps,

of hide and seek on grassy streets,
and darkness ringed with laughter.

Our smiles are wide,
and we are lean and brown, forever.

At Waitangi

My brother sat in a bright morning
of bush and sea.

The water was green and deep
beneath him.

The legs of the jetty slid
slish, slish,

against the sigh
and salt of the tide.

*

Rain waited
behind an island.

The eye of his pipi
swayed beneath a wave.

His happy summer
of rock pools,

shellfish,
and curious pieces of glass

was scattered
across the bay.

*

He held his breath.
'Something's taking

the bait,' he said,
tightening the line,

taking the strain,
standing

and raising his small
rod, sharply.

*

Had he caught
a T-shirt?

a piece of driftwood
passing by?

a sneaker
heavy with sand?

a tangled shadow
of seaweed?

*

His back bent.
He held the purr

of his plastic reel,
the sunlit flash

of his varnished rod,
the lively dance

of his nylon line
in the braided

weight of the sea.
He was a boy

in a bright
green morning,

a man
in his shiny day.

Tide line

You slept on,
as tense

as the night's
arrival,

barely visible
beneath your

randomly patterned
gown,

unaware of the inky
obligations

of the blackbird
on one shoulder.

*

From time
to time,

startled
by a machine's bleep

your eyes opened
and you lifted

an arm,
adjusting the slope

of your neck
and recovering

the familiar,
unreserved tilt

of your head.
A nurse paused

to computerise
your vital signs,

while I filled
a bowl

with lemongrass
refreshed water,

sponged
your forehead,

streamed your restless
fingers

and wrists,
and waited for

your laboured
breathing to ease

within
the deepening

sleep
and territorial

release
of the bird's

rhythmic
'clink, clink'.

Emotional clarity

On Christmas Day
we awoke, as usual,

to disputes over slice-
sizing of the fruit cake

and sherry trifle and
underwhelming gestures

in the Lucky Dip
beneath the tree,

where whistles replicated
the hoots of bugles

and owls, and a tinkling
bowl was purported

to have brushed away
the melodic dust

in which it was found
as it prized itself out

of the ground. Central
to this year's assembly

were oval cakes of sandal
soap celebrating a century

of dedication to complexion
care made famous by

the Government Soap Factory,
Bangalore, as noted

in the rosy glow of its
clientele's blemish-free,

sandalwood-scented skin.
Gift-wrapped in copies

of 'Brise Marine'—
Joseph Brodsky's poem

marking age-related
boundaries of memory

and imagination and
speculating on distance—

the poetic soaps disclosed
Brodsky's desire, as he

composed and smoked,
wreathed in the seaweed

pungency of an ebb tide,
that cosmic energy, coupled

with cosmetic good fortune,
would enable his once-beloved,

Marina, to forever
'remain free of wrinkles'.

Art speak

Welcome to my exhibition
featuring the rich, rolling

purr of a cheetah, as the animal
roamed freely between

sunset's darkening shrubs
on an African savannah.

*

The tonal rumblings were
recorded by an award-

winning sound cameraman,
with veterinary expertise

and sedation supplied
by a stall holder in the local

market. The quality
of the cheetah's timbre

and the financial depth
of the bitcoin transaction

were impressive: the latter
tipping the antique bronze

lion-shaped measuring
weight over the official heroin

and crude opium tical price
index. Publicly heard for

the first time at the opening
of the gallery's initial

postmodern art affair for
the year, the sounds of the only

large cat that purrs, and swiftest
land animal on earth, have

attracted discerning buyers:
with its ebony markings

highlighting a glister
of gold, the cheetah's physical

magnificence has placed
the popularity of pet portraiture

on a par with royalty
in the art-buying heartland.

Time-distant

Another country.
Another platform.

Another continuously peopled dream
over the rim of a teacup.

*

I exhaled.
'The couchettes are too basic!

I can't sleep in a six-person compartment.
This is what I get for booking online

in haste,
in French.

I shall have to cancel,
reschedule,

book a private car—
by which I mean

a sleeper—
with an attendant

to convert the seat
into a bed

and serve coffee and rolls
in the morning.'

*

A white train jolted
in from a siding,

flying flags fore and aft:
a train reserved for the most afflicted,

the most loved,
the ones chosen for the most

miraculous cures,
the first of fourteen transportations

time to leave for Lourdes
after dusk.

Pilgrims, apparently in good health,
drinking beer and lemonade

in a refreshment room,
vacated their small tables.

At the goods entrance,
bearers cleared paths for stretchers

and hand carts.
Mid-platform, porters tidied heaps

of pillows and pallets
and handed out bottles

for filling with
preternatural water.

Cups and bowls,
trays of bread,

containers of broth,
oil stoves

and medicine chests
shuttled past on trolleys,

followed by piles of devotional
books in barrows.

'Attention! Attention!
Please do not block the platform:

Keep the way open for the speedy
passage of patients!'

*

I stood back from the lines
as the train clanked into position.

*

Organisers wearing the scarlet cross
of the Pilgrimage directed the wild

rush into ticketed squares.
A young man, pale and shivering,

was carried past on a stretcher,
formal card of hospitalisation

around his neck.
'Chalk,' he said,

'my tablets taste like chalk.'
An elderly woman

wrapped in a nondescript rug
trundled by in a hand cart,

leaning on an elbow,
a basin at her feet.

'Where is the carriage?
Why must I travel like this?

Why risk the sick headache
the journey brings on?'

A gentleman, otherwise in his prime,
wiped his brow and clutched

the attendant pushing his chair.
'Please, gently lift my leg to the left.'

He turned to a fellow traveller.
'My hip is being torn from me.

Pain penetrates my whole being.
It has become as natural as breathing.'

Another passenger asked him,
'Is this your first trip?'

'My third.
And you?'

'My second.
I accompany a brother

who has ulcers
and will bathe in the pools.'

'Where will you shelter?'
'In a hotel,

a private home,
a hut,

a tent, if the fields are dry,
wherever the sisters suggest.'

*

Queues formed.
Auxiliaries distributed sputum mugs

and folding stools,
adjusted pillows,

covered suppurations
with wads of lint and gauze.

*

From the step of a third-class
carriage, a call:

'Can someone please pass us our young one?'
The child lay in a narrow,

shallow box on wheels,
her eyes closed,

her hair, spared by the illness,
a halo.

She was barely aware of the priest
and white-bibbed Sister of Assumption

who carried her
to a crowded compartment

and placed her,
between parcels and cases,

at her parents' feet.
'She's been wasting for seven years, Sister.'

'Do you have sufficient food for the journey?
Could she manage milk, cheese, a few grapes?'

*

Bernadette appears,
held aloft,

in a dark dress,
kneeling.

'It's the only portrait taken from real life.
She had beautiful feet,

they spoke of her purity.'
'You are?' I asked.

'Elodie.
I sketched the first train as it came in.

Tomorrow I will add the colours:
white takes a long time to dry.

I travel with my neighbour,
who has forgotten how to see and speak.'

'Can she hear?'
'Only music.

She lives in a musty room
with a towel over her head.

I am bringing her
into the open.'

*

Whistles blew.
A last-minute physician,

black bag in hand,
accompanied the stationmaster

to the front of the train.
'So, Ferrand, we meet again.

Did you hear about last season's cure,
the first for years?

I am writing a pamphlet about it.'
'Lourdes has caught on well, sir.

The question is, will it last?'
'Healing takes time, Ferrand.

Everyone who visits the Sanctuary
carries seeds of relief home with them.'

*

I wondered, should I surrender
my passport until disembarkation?

Reset my watch?
Count down the stops?

Listen assiduously to each announcement
as I neared my destination,

prepared to leave promptly,
because Lourdes

is not the end
of the journey?

*

Bells rang.
Signals worked.

Steam gathered.
Iron rattled and grinded.

The train slid out of the station
and disappeared into the tawny

heat of high summer,
windows closed against the breeze.

Ground report

In rising light,
the familiar form
was still on the skyline,

secured by ropes
to the fence posts
and minor trees

that had moderated
recent gales, despite
advice to release

the moorings and allow
the pressured trunk
to arc and sway free.

*

A letter arrived.
'I'm lighting my white
pine-scented candle,'

wrote a friend, and I
paused to wonder
if, in the 'wisdom of crowds',

there was knowledge
of the gleaming
solace of candles?

*

Another correspondent,
also captured by
respect for the pine's

resilience, wrote,
'I believe the tree
watches you as closely

as you watch the tree—
as you move its rigid
image around in your mind,

slaking and assuaging
past and forthcoming
intentions and traumas.'

*

As the day advanced,
arborists in hi-vis vests
and hard hats

manipulated chainsaws,
while a calibrated system
of pulleys and ropes

reduced the pine
to a bare ten-metre stump.
With each section

thrown to the ground,
the fellers whistled
and yelled.

There was a rhythm
going now.
Plumes of sawdust,

calling in light-sprung
atoms and particles
of invisible energy,

danced in shafts of sun
before dispersal
and return to the universe.

*

I leant against
the fernery's wall
of warm stone,

watched a lizard
run for cover,
and a wētā

with spiked legs,
rarely seen during
the day, climb down

from the ponga's
curled heart
and crawl methodically

over the brickwork
and moist soil
of its threshold.

I shaded my eyes
and scanned
the surrounding foliage

for the pine's
tenacious replacement.
Would the active

young fir laden
with bristles and limbs,
gaining height

on the far bank
of the stream,
be a tree for all seasons?

Dear life

After years of shiny leaves
and perfectly proportioned fruit,

the lemon tree was ailing.
Leaf loss bared its branches.

Lemons, although unblemished,
dropped early.

There was more dead wood
than there needed to be.

*

I checked for aphids,
blisters and cracked bark.

Shook the trunk to release
unwanted caterpillars and whiteflies.

*

Internet remedies abounded:
a dose of Epsom salts;

slow-release blood, bone and potash;
a scattering of grass clippings;

a good pruning;
insertion of a nail

through the inner stem
to counteract copper deficiency.

*

I opted to water the small tree
by hand, at its base,

so that relief would speed
straight to its roots.

Sleave of care

1

There is no sound
in the forest,

night or day.
No memory of sound—

whether seasonal anticipation
of the salt

and bread celebrations
of Saturnalia,

the solstices,
or name days

of saints
and martyrs;

no recall
of the comforting,

softly plausible rhythms
of rain,

sun and wind
at dawn

after the balm
of sleep

has untangled
and knitted up

the stressed yarns
of the sleave of care

in soulful,
soundless,

neatened
repairs of sleep.

*

Neither do I hear
fluted notes,

trills or quavers
from the parched

bills of song thrushes
and warblers,

the ground rustle
of insects

in twig cities,
the buzz

and industry
of bees and cicadas.

*

A purple and blue
swamphen pecks

at a patch
of dark earth,

and a pair of ravens
inspect the heft

and weave
of a puzzling

arrangement
of limp leaves.

The stream, swollen
by rain,

splashes the footbridge,
washing away

the sycamore's store
of winged seeds,

irrespective of the need
for the composure

and patience
of nature

when relinquishing,
to the balm

of soundless sleep,
the untangling

of ravelled yarn
into a stable

continuous thread.
Not even the piercing

whistle of a golden
eagle—the Ukrainian

steppe raptor of fever
dreams that forages

on forest floors,
preys in pairs,

and follows few rules—
is apparent.

2

I move slowly over
the forest floor

letting the weight
of the day fall

to the brush of trees
and thickening shrubs:

the maidenhairs—
cossetted ginkgo

once courtyard
saplings in China;

sun-spun pollen
from the hazel's

soft catkins;
the reach and clutch

of winter-bitten
camellias,

and newly grafted
branchlings

on light-starved elms
at the heart

of the forest
where the foliage

is pale and thin,
but the going is easy

in an absence
of underbrush;

*

where there are yews
and spruces that have

never been trimmed,
and oaks so dark

they might almost
be purple;

*

where storms have opened
spaces in the canopy

enabling fallen trees
to remain within

the strengthening reach
of the sun:

ancient trees,
mature trees,

all-but-complete trees,
species sought abroad

by ancestors
and transported

over land
and by sea,

their trunks padded
with soft cloths

beneath hemp,
burlap,

or bazaar-woven
rugs:

horizontal on
ox wagons,

or bound upright
to beams in cargo

hatches and holds—
one tree and beam

tied with nautical knots
to the next,

upper branches
and crowns

waving loosely above
deck on reduced

rivers and easy seas,
restless in air-tasting

winds and drenching
tropical gales,

roots tightly confined
in the breathable

weave of wet sacking,
entire plant support

systems floating
like forest ships

in convoy along
Baltic and Black Sea

coasts, to be winched
ashore like milled

lumber, positioned
width-ways

and covered with canvas
on flag-flying wagons,

*

fit to rumble through
tented fields of thick

winter mud,
the sky-induced brightness

of spring green,
steppe-swept summer

haystacks and grains,
flocks of weather-wise hawks,

mercenary gulls,
and, hunting in pairs

but flying alone,
the golden,

brown-headed
eagles from caves

in the Carpathian Mountains,
riding drifts

of crisp air and spit-
roasted meats

to the ancestral lands
and seasonal pavilions

of the Polish Ukraine.

3

The silence holds,
beyond the forest

and landscape,
as gardeners race

to release the oxen,
unload the wagons,

and slide the cargo
into excavations

higher and wider
than houses

according to predicted
growth,

root spread,
leaf drop,

and individual
blooming capacity;

*

gardeners who scope each plant
for bruising

by hail or heavy rain,
as they run,

shouldering bolts
of shade cloth

and frost cloth,
pausing only to lodge

propagation locations
and processes

with the keepers
of each estate's

Ledger and Schedule of Names.
The hurricane lamps'

sturdy glow
bobs and sways

as large plants are
draped, and coverings

for smaller species
are stretched

and pegged,
corner to corner.

4

With the skies calm,
the plantings secure

and the wagons retired,
the sun rises

to a quietude
of open-throated

bell ringing
and bird song.

*

If exuberance
is anticipated,

gunny sacks of crystals
from the Sea of Azov's

salt marshes
and lagoons

will be dispersed
along the park's

slanting shadows
and winding sleigh

ways—where densities
of drifting sleep

meet lakeside shores
in salted pretences

of snow,
and mounds

of withered sedges,
long-stemmed eelgrasses,

and salt carts en route
from shallow

and sub-tidal coves,
arrive in the placid light

of the hour
before dawn,

to idle
and await easement

of the distracted stresses
and threads

in the silent dramas
of a dream

that is always the same.

Notes and acknowledgements

Epigraph (p. 8)
Marcus Aurelius, *Meditations: A New Translation with an Introduction by Gregory Hays* (The Modern Library, 2002), Book 7, p. 88. The context is that of change: 'Frightened of change? But what can exist without it? What's closer to nature's heart? Can you take a hot bath and leave the firewood as it was? Eat food without transforming it? Can any vital process take place without something being changed?'

'Heartfelt' (p. 11)
'transfer to critical care in the city': A condition known as Intensive Care Unit delirium—a potentially preventable and reversible delirium, characterised by confusion and other disturbances of consciousness and cognition—can develop in intensive care unit patients.

'echoes and reverberations' is a reference to echocardiograph imaging, i.e. a visual cardiac ultrasound of the heart in motion.

'*Papaver somniferum*' (p. 28)
'Aunti Emma' is a street name for opium (*Papaver somniferum*).

'Amor fati' (p. 33)
The title refers to the Stoic philosophic mindset, defined as the love or embrace of fate, or of that which is necessary.

Mention of Seneca, Epictetus and Emperor Marcus Aurelius in this poem recalls the three foremost stoics of theism.

The poem concerns a brown trout, said to have belonged to the Scottish driver of a steam locomotive. The fish accompanied the driver on his daily journey between Edinburgh and London for over ten years, travelling in the 'interior of a railway engine', and staying in the driver's overnight 'digs'. ('Fishes of the Rivers', *The Children's Encyclopedia*, Volume Seven, originated and edited by Arthur Mee.)

'From the Stoa' (p. 43)
This poem recalls the Painted Hall at Athens, known as the 'Stoa', or Porch, c.310 BCE, where lectures on Stoicism were given.

'Cautious optimism' (p. 56)
'Ejection fraction' is a cardiac term denoting the percentage of blood that remains in the heart's left ventricle after each ventricular contraction.

'Sleave of care' (p. 89)
The title is a phrase from *Macbeth*, Act 2, Scene 2, in which a 'sleave', as a

yarn, or a mass of silk or wool, constitutes an entanglement of stress and care, eased by the balm of sleep.

My poem is unrelated to *Macbeth*; rather, it evokes world-famous Park Sofjyivka, near the town of Uman in Ukraine, from prose extracts, factually based and imagined, in my novel *The Fountain of Tears* (Victoria University Press, 2006). The garden was created by Felix General Stanislaw Szczesny Potocki (1751–1805) as a 'love park' for his wife, Sofia Konstantinovna Potocka (1801–1875). In 1811, a lyrical guide in verse was composed for the park's opening by Polish Enlightenment Poet Laureate, Stanislaw Trembecki (1739–1812). In 2004, the world-famous landscaped garden, known as the Tsarina's Garden following the 1832 confiscation of the Potocki properties by the Tsar, was renamed, and has remained, the Ukrainian National Dendrological Park, 'Sofiyivka'.

*

Acknowledgements are due to the editors of publications in which early versions of selected poems in this collection first appeared, including adaptations from untitled prose.

'Allurement' was first published as 'Letter', in *We Set Out One Morning: Works from the BNZ Art Collection* by Gregory O'Brien and Peter Thodley (Private Bank of New Zealand, 2006).

'Imperium' was adapted from untitled prose in *Communicating Pain: Exploring Suffering through Language, Literature and Creative Writing* (Routledge Advances in the Medical Humanities, 2019).

The final line of 'Emotional clarity' appears in 'Brise Marine' by Joseph Brodsky, as published in Brodsky's *So Forth [Poems]* (Hamish Hamilton, 1996).

'At Waitangi' was first published as 'Boy Fishing', in *Jewels in the Water*, ed. Terry Locke (Leaders Press, University of Waikato, 2000).

'The far north' was the winner of the Lancome Poetry Competition, 1998, and published as 'The Two of Us in Our Togs', *NZ Woman's Weekly*, 7 September 1998.

Versions of 'Time–distant' were adapted from the narrative poem 'White Train, as published in *How Does It Hurt?* (Victoria University Press, 2014), and informed by Émile Zola's novel *Lourdes*; also published in *Communicating Pain*.

'Ground report' was adapted from untitled prose published in *Communicating Pain*.

'Dear life' was adapted from untitled prose published in *How Does It Hurt?* and *Communicating Pain*.